2021
and me

Written and Illustrated by Sue Dower

Published in 2022 by Susan Dower

© Copyright Susan Dower

ISBN: 978-1-913898-26-7

Book & Cover Design by Russell Holden

 Pixel Tweaks Publications
SELF PUBLISHING MADE SIMPLE

www.pixeltweakspublications.com

All illustrations © Copyright Susan Dower

A Catalogue record for this book is available from the British Library.

Printed by Ingram

The story of one person's journey through another difficult year.

I knew it could only get better,

So, I pinned all my hopes onto 2021,

It tried hard but, in the end, it just didn't deliver,

The disappointment's still there; it's not gone…

CONTENTS

January 2021

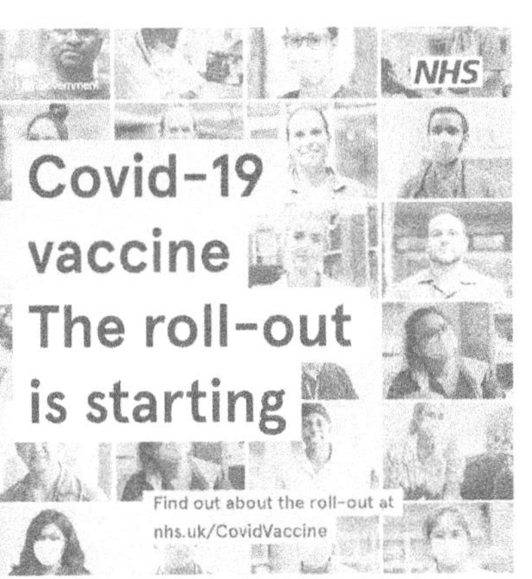

ONE DAY

I finished 2020 flat on my bottom,
That sums it up for me; what do you think?
The temperature had dropped, the ground was frozen over,
So, I became Jayne Torvill, in a crude ice-skating rink.

My problem was, I'd not attended the rehearsals,
My technique was suspect, the choreography as well,
I tried desperately to stay upright and look graceful,
But I'm afraid I missed the double axel and just fell.

I really thought that I showed some early promise,
In fact, at first, I could have earned a perfect ten,
But my performance began to fall away quite badly,
As I clung to railings and passing lamp posts now and then.

I was a few yards from my house, I nearly made it,
I could hear Ravel's Bolero in my ear,
But I celebrated too soon on the crescendo,
Now I have bruises; quite a start to the New Year.

FOUR DAYS

A new year, and the situation's no better,
A new strain of Covid, is causing us stress,
A new announcement, the Government is worried,
A new message saying, we're still in a mess.

A new threat level installed, it's up to five now,
A new set of restrictions, to cause me some grief,
A new lockdown, it's the third one and counting,
A new Oxford vaccine, and yet, no relief.

Just like me, the Tory rebels are angry,
We are in lockdown, and it's like Hampton Court Maze,
We need directions, so we can locate the exit,
As it is, we're wandering around, in a daze.

Just like me, the Tory rebels have questions,
How do we find the way out? What is the plan?
Will we take the vaccine route? Is that the best path?
What percentage must we achieve, before we can?

Just like me, the Tory rebels are despondent,
With the school closure U-turn and exams on hold,
The impact these decisions have on life chances,
Will be visible for years to come, we are told.

Just like me, the Tory rebels are frustrated,
They want exit targets and a time frame, right now!
They want to return to a degree of normality,
They want answers to the 'Why? When? and How?

TWELVE DAYS

I'm waiting for the end of the tulip season,
Boris said that's when restrictions might ease,
I'm hoping it's soon, but when is that?
Could someone just let me know, please?

I've had enough of tier four, it's a challenge,
There are days, when I think, 'What the hell'…
I'll break that rule, I really can't take it,
But I'm being watched, yes, I mean it, I can tell.

COVID patrols have appeared on the streets now,
The police have toughened their stance, there's no doubt,
They used to Engage, Explain, Encourage, before Enforcing,
But that 'Four E System', perhaps, is on its way out.

On the spot fines are being issued more often,
I'm not allowed to 'mingle', have a picnic or leave the town,
I'm not allowed to visit other households, or see my family,
I can't have a meal out as hospitality's closed down.

So, I'll wait patiently 'til the tulips are blooming,
What! We've not had the crocuses, or daffodils, yet,
I'll have to pin my hopes on some early flowerings,
I'll cross my fingers; that won't work, you can bet…

SIXTEEN DAYS

I am still waiting for my vaccination,
My daughter's had hers, she's front line,
Three million people have now received it,
But I don't know yet, when I'll get mine.

I'm in a priority group, so I'm hopeful,
I'm not way down the list, that I know,
The Government say that they have a target,
Mid-February; so just a few weeks to go.

Wait a minute, an NHS letter on my doormat,
Could this be my appointment, let me see?
No! It's a bowel cancer test kit, just what I needed,
Now, I'll be scraping poo into a tube, oh dear me!

They've just told me today is 'Blue Monday',
I'm supposed to be depressed, I didn't know,
I thought it was the consequence of lockdown,
But apparently, it seems, I should be feeling low.

There's me, thinking it was the lack of social contact,
The dearth of culture and the tedium of routine,
Whereas really, it's just the time of year that's caused it,
That's their theory! I have my own, know what I mean?

TWENTY-FOUR DAYS

I had my vaccination on Friday, it came early,
Because the boosters have been delayed, to 'spread the net',
So, fifty per cent protection is what I'm offered,
Instead of ninety, but I'll take what I can get.

My body didn't like it, I can tell you,
I had a sore arm, pain in my head, and muscle ache,
There was a tiredness which was threatening to overwhelm me,
I was exhausted, and I could not stay awake.

So, yesterday came and went, I didn't notice,
I slept most of the afternoon, I couldn't choose,
It wasn't my decision, I was forced to take it,
Another day gone; one I can't afford to lose.

TWENTY-SIX DAYS

The Vaccine Minister has issued a warning,
'Don't book a summer holiday abroad', don't you dare!
I was deprived of foreign travel last year, but was hopeful,
Now, the disappointment is really difficult to bear.

'Looks like it's Bognor again, dear', is the news headline,
I suppose that is the stance I should take,
Shrug the shoulders, 'suck it up', just accept it,
It, certainly won't matter, how many protests I make.

In his statement Mr Zahawi said there is progress,
We're vaccinating faster than other countries, that is true,
But on our journey, we have only just 'reached base camp',
And there's a long way to go, before we're through.

So, my passport will stay unopened, in its wallet,
Unvisited countries, on my list to see, will still remain,
I'll tidy my holiday drawer, check my ear plugs and my sun cream,
And look forward to when I'm travelling again.

TWENTY-NINE DAYS

I'm wearing my granddaughter's pyjamas,
An unwanted Christmas present, so she gave them to me,
They fit nicely, I was pleased, and then I noticed,
The 'Merry, Merry,' message on the front, for all to see,

That's not the word I'd use to describe me at the moment,
There are others I could choose; that one's not right,
But, the irony of it made me smile, I couldn't help it,
And I'll be wearing them in bed, again, tonight.

THIRTY-FIVE DAYS

Professor Whitty was slightly up-beat this morning,
He's talked to his colleagues and they seem to agree,
That we're past the peak of this second wave; they think so,
Could restrictions be eased a little earlier? We'll see…

Ten million people have now received the vaccine,
And it is proving that it does curb the spread,
The number of positive tests is declining,
It still is high, but there might be light now up ahead.

Boris says they will 'chart a way out of the lockdown',
So, if I add this news to my premium bond win,
And forget about the puncture I had yesterday,
I could convince myself that better days will soon begin.

I've been binge-watching the Australian Open,
I didn't mean to, but I got carried away,
Before I knew it, my recording was over,
I'd seen the whole of the first day of play.

What a treat it was, I really enjoyed it,
I have few pleasures at this time, so it felt good,
To indulge myself in something I value,
It made me feel brighter, I didn't realise it could.

There were a few close matches and inevitably, some upsets,
Quarantine issues meant some players weren't match fit,
There'd been complaints, but on the whole, there was acceptance,
Against the odds, the event was happening, get on with it!

But, if I think about it, it wasn't just the tennis,
It was the near normality of it all that lifted me,
The spectators in the stands, sitting close together,
And Jo Durie's commentary, full of positivity.

I could absorb the atmosphere in the arena, as I once did,
No recorded cheering, no canned applause, this time, it's real,
The play much improved because of crowd participation,
Yes, this is exactly, how I remember it used to feel.

FORTY-THREE DAYS

That'll teach me to be optimistic,
Thinking the situation will soon be alright,
One positive case out in Melbourne,
And things took a turn for the worse overnight.

The city is now in full lockdown,
The State borders are closed and shut tight,
The Government's permitting the tennis to continue,
But no spectators are allowed on the site.

Another disappointment to add to my list now,
It's becoming difficult to take blow after blow,
I'm being pummelled into submission, that's what it feels like,
How long will the onslaught go on? I don't know.

FIFTY-FOUR DAYS

I took my vitamin D and glanced at the news headline,
'We're on a one-way road to freedom', I read,
A declaration to encourage, from the Prime Minister,
'The end is really in sight', is what he said.

What do they call that now? Oh yes, it's optimism,
It's been missing for a while but I think it is back,
As he promised us, a better spring and summer,
With an assurance that we're on the right track.

It came with a warning that nothing is certain,
Patience is needed, we mustn't leave lockdown too soon,
'Everyone must play their part' and be prudent,
So, restrictions could be lifted on the twenty-first of June.

Another four months before the exit is completed,
There'll be some improvements before then, so they say,
It will be gradual because the plan is made up of stages,
I might be allowed to hug someone in the middle of May!

But I'm stuck in this time warp for the moment,
Complaining daily but determined to cope,
I'll get my diary out and dust off the cover,
So I can tick the weeks off, now there's a glimmer of hope.

FIFTY-NINE DAYS

Billy Connolly is now my new hero,
I watched a documentary of his, late last night,
I always thought he was probably worthy of admiration,
This programme proved to me, I was, in fact, right.

He told the story of his childhood in Glasgow,
He described the poverty, the deprivation on his street,
He took us through the slum clearance with its dire consequences,
Talked of the indignities, whilst still remaining upbeat.

He outlined the positives, he said there were plenty,
Life was difficult but straightforward, in a way,
There were simple pleasures and lots of time to enjoy them,
He was allowed a freedom, which we often don't have, today.

Probably, as a result, he has a confidence, that's obvious,
He is quick-witted, he can stand alone and entertain,
He's a people-person, a communicator, a story-teller,
And, when he's rude, he'll be forgiven, once again.

Behind it all, there is an intellect, that's hidden,
A love of books and works of art, he had a list,
He spoke of sharing, some of his favourites with others,
To give them pleasure, which they might otherwise have missed.

He is not well now, but he still has a sense of humour,
There's no self-pity, he joked about it, what can I say?
He's a controversial figure, but I like him,
And what I do know is, he brightened up my day.

SIXTY-SEVEN DAYS

I'm fearing for my sanity, I tell you,
They say I can have a coffee with a friend, outside, again,
I suppose I should be grateful for small mercies…
Perhaps I would be, if it wasn't for the rain.

I should be taking my first steps on this 'road to freedom',
As, today, stage one of lockdown exit has begun,
But I'm afraid I'm going nowhere, just as usual,
Social phobia could be an issue, when we're done.

Day after day, week after week, they indoctrinate me,
Stay away from everyone, do not mingle, do not meet,
Do not fraternise, keep your distance, it's relentless,
So much so, I circumnavigate others, in the street!

It's not normal, but over time, like a bad habit or addiction,
It becomes part of your make-up and you cannot let it go,
I'm told to avoid people, they're a threat to me, but when it's over,
Will I continue this mode of behaviour? Surely, no!

For a long time now, I haven't 'done' mirrors,
They're surplus to requirements; extraneous, if that's the right word,
And, if I need to check my appearance, I remove my glasses,
My reflection looks so much better, if it's blurred.

So, imagine how horrific it was for me, on Monday,
In my first Zoom meeting, 'beamed' on the computer screen,
To see myself quite plainly, as others see me,
I was unnerved, a little shocked at what I'd seen.

I moved backwards into the room, so I looked smaller,
I sank down into my chair and tried to disappear,
I crouched into the corner of the screen to try a different angle,
But nothing worked, I was still there, and really clear.

Perhaps it was the lighting, or the position of the camera?
I made some adjustments, but, no way did it improve,
Then came the announcement that we're doing it next week,
Think I'll switch to audio; That might be my best move!

SEVENTY-THREE DAYS

Another Mother's Day, but not one to remember,
Lockdown restrictions mean celebrations are not allowed,
We can't have a meal out as nowhere is open,
Can't meet together at home; that's classed as a crowd.

I had a face-time call with my son, who's in the city,
Better than nothing I suppose, so I pretended I didn't mind,
My daughter invited me to walk with her to Dalton,
That's still legal, so we hoped the weather would be kind.

But, of course, as you might have guessed, it wasn't,
The wind began to buffet us, the drizzle turned to heavy rain,
I kept smiling as I felt the dampness permeating my layers,
But I hope she won't be suggesting it again.

SEVENTY-NINE DAYS

They say disasters come in threes, I really hope not,
Two is enough for me when I'm not feeling great,
I can't stand the upset, the inconvenience and disruption,
It's much too complicated, I'm feeling low, I'm in a state.

I could do without the leak in my extension,
The damp is coming through and is tracking down the wall,
The roofer says it's not his fault, and I believe him,
So, the problem now needs solving, who do I call?

My car's been in the garage for a week now,
I'm 'dead on my feet', I've never walked as much,
There's been some realigning and adjusting, to save me money,
But nothing worked, so they are going to change the clutch!

Hang the expense, I suppose, it doesn't matter,
And, there'll be a solution to my problems, I have to hope,
But I'm struggling, as it is with abnormality,
So extra stress is most unwelcome, I just can't cope.

What I need now is some good news, to lift my spirits,
But no, a third wave in other countries, so I hear,
Our 'road to freedom' might turn out to be a little longer,
Than was anticipated, that's becoming rather clear.

The newspapers are calling it 'Freedom Monday',
An exaggeration, but lockdown's easing, it's a start,
Small gatherings will be allowed in parks and gardens,
And team sport legal, if I want to join in, and take part.

My club's bowling green will be open, with restrictions,
Plans are underway to start the league again in May,
As captain, I have contacted my team members,
It's been a year, so without exception, they want to play.

I've missed the social contact, that is obvious,
But, come tomorrow, I can meet five friends and I can mix,
We'll be outside, but face to face, not on a camera,
And after that, my second vaccination at ten to six.

A 'red-letter day' for me, therefore, tomorrow,
It's been a long time coming, but things are looking good,
With no COVID patients in the hospital, at the moment,
I just need the weather to improve, do you think it could?

EIGHTY-NINE DAYS

I was furious yesterday, that's not unusual,
I can't stand condescension or unwarranted advice,
But the stewards at the vaccination centre didn't know that,
'Mind how you go. Don't want you falling over', that's much too nice!

'Can you manage the stairs? Is that an issue for you?'
'You can stay down here, it's not a problem, it's quite OK',
A stony stare was my reply, and with a determination,
I raced up the steps, two at a time, what can I say?

An overreaction, and very rude, I will admit it,
But, at this time, my tolerance levels are very low,
I have been forced to become self-sufficient, and anti-social,
I am a product of thirteen months of lockdowns; I just know.

NINETY-THREE DAYS

Happy Easter, but please don't enjoy it,
A fourth lockdown will likely follow if you do,
So, don't mingle too much in your parks and gardens,
More doom-laden government advice, so what's new?

They're right to be concerned, there is frustration,
The mass gatherings in city centres are proof it's tough,
To continue to endure the social isolation,
Acts of defiance, to show they've nearly had enough.

The Prime Minister thinks a COVID passport is the answer,
It's controversial, seventy MPs do not agree,
They're using words like discriminatory and divisive,
Authoritarian and un-British; so we'll see.

More than thirty-one million have had a vaccination,
Another five million, like me, have now had two,
But, for those not allowed one for health reasons,
There would be unfair consequences, it's very true…

In the meantime, I'll host a pizza-party on my patio,
I've invited friends, within legal limits, so just a few,
The sun is shining, and the sparkling wine is chilling,
Several glasses and I'll solve the country's problems; I always do.

NINETY-SEVEN DAYS

Non-essential shops and outdoor hospitality open up on Monday,
Gyms and hairdressers too, and camping holidays are allowed,
The F.A. Cup Final will be played with twenty thousand spectators,
And the World Snooker with a full capacity crowd.

We're on the right track, you would think, but wait a minute,
A government statement says 'life won't be normal again this year',
And that, despite the success of the vaccine roll-out,
Scientists think we'll have a third wave; they are quite clear.

I'm sure they told me that I'm on a 'road to freedom',
There's weekly testing and COVID passports are to be used,
But I still can't socialise indoors and must keep my distance,
Whilst mass events are being planned; I'm just confused!

I'm not saying that I've got a problem,
But I'm a little concerned, none the less,
I'm becoming an alfresco-socialiser,
And, if I'm not careful, I might be in a mess.

It's the Government, they're saying it's legal,
I can meet friends outside now, so I do,
But perhaps three times a week is excessive,
As I must visit the pub's beer garden too.

Add all this to dinner dates in my bubble;
I could have alcohol-free days, but I don't,
This afternoon, it's pie and peas and Prosecco,
I should abstain, but, there again, perhaps I won't.

ONE HUNDRED AND FOURTEEN DAYS

Simon Reeve is a travel reporter,
He makes documentary programmes for the BBC,
Present restrictions mean he can't visit 'far-flung' places,
So, he's in the Lake District filming a series of three.

He spent a morning with us at the Women's Centre in Barrow,
His researcher found us on the Town Hall website, no doubt,
He came with his two camera-men and an assistant,
To investigate and find out what we're about.

The atmosphere was relaxed and friendly; that made it easy,
He talked to the Centre Manager at length; the serious bit,
He interviewed one of our 'survivors' and heard her story,
Totally unscripted, I was impressed, I must admit.

They filmed in the community room, the clothes bank, and in drop-in,
He learned about our strategies, courses and the services we give,
We prepared an emergency 'flee-bag' to show him,
As he was concerned about how some women are forced to live.

In the present climate, like other charities, the Centre struggles,
We've lost our lottery money and competition for funding is strong,
There are bids in at the moment but we're not hopeful,
Perhaps some positive publicity might just help us along.

So, thank you Simon Reeve for showing a degree of interest,
Our Housing Officer gave him some hero-worship, to help our case,
She produced his book out of her handbag so he could sign it,
And told him he looked good on camera but even better face to face!

ONE HUNDRED AND TWENTY-THREE DAYS

It's bank holiday Monday and the weather is awful,
Which is a problem when my social life must be outside,
Still, it's the second day of the world snooker final,
I might watch, perhaps I could enjoy it, if I just tried.

There was a capacity crowd, the first time in over a year,
The fans needed a face mask and a negative test,
It meant a sporting event which was somewhere near normal,
So, the players more likely to give of their best.

I'm no expert, but the standard of play was impressive,
The commentators said it was, so I know I was right,
There was high-quality potting and excellent safety,
Now addicted, I'll catch the last session tonight.

The match lived up to the high expectations,
The three-time champion was ahead and continuing to score,
When his opponent started to make a late comeback,
A tense finish; I think I'll come back for more.

ONE HUNDRED AND THIRTY DAYS

We've been so successful in lowering infection rates,
That the Covid alert level has dropped down to three,
There's no question that the next exit stage will happen,
It's due on Monday, we'll see what concessions there will be.

Lockdown and social distancing have done the hard work,
They've been winning the battle to keep infection rates low,
And the vaccine programme has now taken over,
It's fighting the UK virus and ensuring variants don't grow.

The cabinet meets tomorrow morning, to agree the next step,
Michael Gove, says some 'friendly contact' is overdue,
The Health Minister agrees we need some hugs and kisses,
It's been a long time now; we've been deprived; that's nothing new.

I think a slight improvement next week is sounding likely,
If I choose a 'green' country on the Government's list, I could book a cruise,
I could go to my art class, the pub or cinema, have my lunch out,
I could watch my grandson playing rugby; it's all good news.

Experts tell us there are real benefits to hugging,
It reduces blood pressure and lowers stress levels, they say,
For over a year, as I live alone, I have been untouchable,
But that is changing, I can hug someone today.

For a long time now, my world has been a cold place,
No cuddles, no strokes, no pats to help relieve the pain,
No comforting arm around the shoulder to make me feel good,
Now that is over, I can have close contact, once again.

I'm not too excited though, because there are provisos,
Medical officers say I must be cautious and not gung-ho,
I must be selective, keep it short and not too frequent,
Do it outside, turn away; What? Really? I don't know!

ONE HUNDRED AND THIRTY-NINE DAYS

I'm not used to having days you'd class as normal,
But yesterday came close I'm sure you will agree,
I had a meeting with the builder and a dental check-up,
Then my youngest granddaughter came to visit and have tea.

I've not seen her for a while, it's not been easy,
There've been garden visits and chance encounters now and then,
But this week as we're beginning to leave lockdown,
We had some quality time, the first since I don't know when.

We did nothing out of the ordinary or special,
We snuggled up to look at photos and share our news,
We had a McDonald's and then she slaughtered me at 'Dobble',
I tried hard, but she's much too quick, I always lose!

I'm feeling better after that little dose of normal,
So much so, that I will risk it and take some more,
My social life has been constrained but I am hopeful,
That I can resurrect it and enjoy it like before.

ONE HUNDRED AND FORTY-THREE DAYS

I've had to find my diary, I suddenly need it,
It's been totally redundant, now it's not,
There are events, dates and times, that need recording,
A few entries now; in fact, there's quite a lot.

I'm back at my art class and I continue volunteering,
My bowls leagues have recommenced, I'll play all three,
I'm having evenings in the pub and café lunches,
And a coach trip to Carlisle is booked for me.

I'm seeing family and friends, when and where I want to,
I don't have to cancel or postpone because of rain,
So, I'm cautiously optimistic, but not certain,
That I'll be cured and back to 'normal' once again.

The negative effects of lockdown have had an impact,
I've not been able to look ahead, life's been mundane,
Nothing to excite me or enthuse about, just tedium,
It made me apathetic and disinclined to use my brain.

The lack of freedom and isolation also, hurt me,
I have been resentful, cross and intolerant, most every day,
As well as unreasonable, over-sensitive and tearful,
Argumentative; quite anti-social, you might say.

Still, perhaps with prospects of near normality a little brighter,
I can put those adverse traits behind me now,
And look forward to making plans and going places,
I will enjoy myself; let's hope I can remember how!

ONE HUNDRED AND FORTY-NINE DAYS

It's the May bank holiday and, on the surface, all seems normal,
My daughter and her family are at Lowther in their campervan,
I'll meet friends for lunch, walk round the reservoir and through the quarry,
Then Roland Garros starts, I'll watch some matches; that's my plan.

The weather forecast's good, I can spend time on my garden,
I watched Monty Don, my inspiration, on TV last night,
There's a list of jobs he recommends I try this weekend,
I must get on with that as well, he's always right.

I'll do some shopping with my granddaughter on Sunday,
We'll buy a sandwich, stroll down the canal to reach the sea,
My sister-in-law will cook my tea and make me drink Prosecco,
As I said, all very normal, so, what's bothering me?

Life is definitely more acceptable, there is no question,
Boris says lockdown exit is irreversible, but is that true?
Scientists are advising caution because of variants, it's unsettling,
I'm trying to be positive, but it's not an easy thing to do.

Now I've had a taste of near normality I don't want to lose it,
I'm fighting the uncertainty and apprehension, I'm sure I'll win,
Less than a month now 'til the promised end of all restrictions,
I've got to hope that then, the rest of my life, can begin.

Well, Freedom Monday is not happening, I might have known it,
A month's delay and then they'll consider it again,
It's not cancelled, just postponed, thanks to the Delta variant,
Which has led to caution as it's a more infectious strain.

I am 'out and about' now, so life is bearable,
My week is full, I'm doing something every day,
But I'm not totally relaxed, there's an underlying sadness,
I can't explain why, but I'm not happy, that's all I'll say.

Still, Wimbledon is being played this year, thank goodness,
The football Euros are taking place now, as I speak,
Both events are fan pilots with strict capacity limits lifted,
Despite no lockdown exit, as expected, early on next week.

We're making progress you could say, but I'm impatient,
It's been fifteen months now. I've had enough, what can I do?
When will I be able to act on impulse without considering restrictions?
Some experts think it could be in the spring of 2022!

Matt Hancock has resigned; yet another scandal,
Covid rules broken during an extra-marital affair,
The Health Minister breaching regulations, can you believe it?
Unacceptable behaviour, once again, I just despair.

On the plus side, his replacement is Sajid Javid,
There's a change in tone, there's optimism, he's offering hope,
He says he's confident that in July, we'll be back to normal,
Curbs will be lifted; we'll contain the virus and we'll cope.

I'll choose to believe him, because, of course, that's what I'm wanting,
His parliamentary statement was convincing, and so was he,
When lockdown ends, it's irreversible, he promised,
Roll on the nineteenth, two weeks to go and then we're free…

Lockdown is over and it's another 'Freedom Monday',
It came just in time as my patience was wearing thin,
Schools are out and we're enjoying warmer weather,
A 'natural firebreak' to allow some normality to begin.

That's what Boris said, but he still was urging caution,
As infections rise at a rate of thirty thousand every day,
He informed us that the Pandemic is far from over,
But that we must fight it in a slightly different way.

So, as promised, legal restrictions have been lifted,
Now, there's a shift in guidance for us, the public at large,
The state will no longer be responsible for our behaviour,
Instead, company bosses and we, ourselves, will be in charge.

The message is; continue to be sensible and wary,
Don't totally dispense with face masks, and be careful in a crowd,
Be ready to produce proof of immunity or vaccination,
As we venture further afield, now that it is allowed.

I am determined to be optimistic and not worry,
I still don't seek out depressing figures, I don't want to know,
But I couldn't avoid the latest news this morning,
The new Health Minister has tested positive. A bit of a blow!

TWO HUNDRED AND FOUR DAYS

The NHS Covid App is causing problems, I just knew it,
I wouldn't download it, it's a privacy matter, it's not for me,
Restrictions were bad enough without being under supervision,
My whereabouts known, my every move noted, not totally free.

As the infection rate rises again, it's becoming very active,
It means enforced isolation if you are contacted and your device 'pings',
It's happening so often, it's starting to overwhelm us,
They're calling it 'pingdemonium', a 'pingdemic', amongst other things.

Up to a million people this week are affected,
That figure is double what it was the week before,
They can't go to work so many businesses are suffering,
The retail sector, pubs and factories, and many more.

The CBI says staff shortages are a risk to our recovery,
Supermarkets warn of gaps on the shelves, perhaps no beer, perhaps no bread,
Ambulance and Police chiefs say response times are being affected,
But Boris is adamant he won't change the system, that's what he said.

So, emergency plans have been announced: something must happen,
They involve special exemption for lorry drivers with a negative test,
Factory workers and police are also included, but for us others,
Press the delete button on your phone, that's probably best.

I am an emotional wreck, I'm in pieces,
I'm watching the Olympics, I don't know if I'll survive,
I find myself sobbing each time a Briton wins a medal,
Sixteen times so far and it's only day five.

Plus, there's the agony of the near misses, it's nerve wracking,
So many fourth places, it's very difficult to bear,
A hundredth of a second, a fingertip and it's over,
A sudden death tie-break, just two points to win it; it's just not fair!

Every breakfast time, I am glued to the catchup programme,
I thought the 'The Games' would fail because of Covid, it's true,
But, despite restrictions, 'bubbles', masks and empty stadia,
The athletes are producing, doing just what they're supposed to do.

So many stories of dedication and commitment,
Overcoming obstacles and adversities along the way,
I'm full of admiration, of the fortitude and determination,
Sport can shape an individual, for the better, I have to say.

TWO HUNDRED AND TWENTY DAYS

The Women's Centre in Barrow is now, well established,
And, I can say, it is close to my heart,
My Soroptimist friend asked me to join them,
In setting it up; so, I was there, right at the start.

That was eight years ago, the first one in the county,
There were women with issues needing support to help them get through,
I wasn't arrogant enough to think I could make a difference,
But I'd work in the background and do as much as I could do.

We've come a long way since our shaky beginning,
Four trustees, one member of staff and a few people like me,
Housed in rooms with leaking ceilings and smelly toilets,
Clothes bank in a cupboard, but that's how it had to be.

From a client base of nil, we now have seven hundred,
Despite funding problems, we continue to exist,
Over the years volunteers have come and gone, that is expected,
But there's a dedicated group and you can add me to that list.

I don't give my time to be rewarded; it's enough to feel valued,
Prize-giving ceremonies leave me cold, I must admit,
But, on Friday, when we received the Queen's Award for volunteering,
I was delighted, I accepted gladly, I'm proud of it!

The Olympics are over and I have withdrawal symptoms,
I am deflated, I am bereft, I'm feeling low,
I'd got used to a daily dose of sporting drama,
I was addicted, totally dependent, I just know.

I suppose I should be grateful that they happened,
It was a controversial decision to go ahead,
Staged during a global pandemic, unprecedented,
Protestors campaigning to the bitter end, reporters said.

But the world was Covid-weary, and needed lifting,
The challenges seemed unsurmountable, it's true,
Yet, the Japanese hosts were very resilient and defiant,
And, against all the odds, sport won, and they got through.

No vibrant, joyous atmosphere like in Rio.
No crowds, like at the Euros, where fans filled every seat,
Instead, harsh rules, endless restrictions and daily testing,
Competitors in fear of being 'pinged', and unable to compete.

So, an anxious and stressful situation, that's for certain,
But the athletes overcame it all and saved the day,
Impressive performances and inspirational stories,
Made it a classic Games, the best yet, I have to say.

TWO HUNDRED AND TWENTY-SEVEN DAYS

I just looked at the news headlines, then wished I hadn't,
There seems to be gloom and doom everywhere that I turn,
The Taliban is waging war in South Asia,
Whilst in Europe, wildfires are continuing to burn.

Japan has had heavy rain, followed by landslides,
Haiti has had an earthquake with hundreds of dead,
In India, lightning strikes are killing the population,
Hard to believe, I know, but that's what I read.

The scientists, as usual, succeed in making me worry,
The extremes of weather are caused by climate change, they say,
We're running out of time to halt its progress, they are warning,
Humanity is in code red and global warming seems here to stay.

They've upset me in the past with Covid forecasts and predictions,
Their fact that the new variants might be vaccine-resistant, I'll ignore,
I'll accept my booster If and when it's offered, and my flu jab,
Pneumonia, Shingles and any other preventative, what's more.

TWO HUNDRED AND FORTY-SEVEN DAYS

My granddaughter had a baby on Thursday,
He took a long time to arrive but is well worth the wait,
The members of my family all have changes in status,
And, of course, I myself, am now officially, 'great'.

Secretly, I must admit, I did suspect it,
And, at last it is confirmed; it must be true,
But, wait, aren't people with that title usually ancient?
Think they might be, so just call me Nanna Sue.

41

Three quarters of the year has gone and, still, I'm not happy,
My situation is not as I'd want it to be,
I can't regain control because of limitations and restrictions,
I'm living my life through other people's; that's not like me.

Recently, I visited New York, without leaving Barrow,
Before that, I was in Tokyo, not once, but twice,
I entered every event in the Olympics, with our athletes,
Then I went on court with Emma Raducanu; she seems nice.

I felt the joy of her victory and celebrated,
I felt her opponent's frustration, missing out, when oh so near,
I felt pride in her history-making achievement,
Again, I lived it, perhaps too involved; that's very clear,

That's how it is, things could be worse, but summer's ending,
The Government's introduced its Covid winter measures, so we'll see,
The A Scheme, seems OK, relying totally on vaccinations,
Let's hope it works because I really don't fancy Plan 'B'.

TWO HUNDRED AND SEVENTY-SIX DAYS

As summer fades, business leaders are worried,
There are labour shortages, due to Covid and Brexit combined,
Too few lorry drivers to supply our pumps with petrol,
And hospitality staff are very difficult to find.

The food processing industry is struggling,
Not enough workers in the factories, they're just not there,
They're predicting there'll be no turkeys for Christmas,
Still, as a vegetarian, that's no bother, I don't care!

I'm faced with empty shelves when I go shopping,
I'll do without what is not there and not complain,
Petrol is rationed at the garage, the queues are endless,
So, how do I get to Ulverston for my booster? I'll go by train!

TWO HUNDRED AND NINETY-TWO DAYS

I'm double vaccinated and now, I am 'boosted',
Does that make me invincible? I hardly think so,
It doesn't seem to matter what the level of protection,
The virus can strike at will, as infection rates show.

Here, in Barrow, we are struggling to contain it,
We're third in the league table. That wasn't the plan,
Over four hundred people tested positive last week,
Cases amongst youngsters, the highest since figures began.

Depressing news once more, it's never ending,
But there are highlights in my life, which are easier to bear,
Watching my grandson score the winning try in rugby,
Through to the final at Craven Park now; I'll be there!

Coming from behind to win our club quiz was amazing,
The favourites stunned in second place with everyone aware,
In a depleted team, as well, so ego-boosting,
I felt triumphant and it showed, but I don't care.

I took baby for a walk and enjoyed the sunshine,
I received a present from a client, she said I'd been kind,
I started plans for foreign travel in the springtime,
I's been so long that I'll go anywhere, I don't mind.

I am still wary and I'm avoiding crowded places,
But hopefully, next year, there'll be no need to take fright,
I have registered to get tickets for the Laver Cup in London,
That's in September. Will I get there? I think I might!

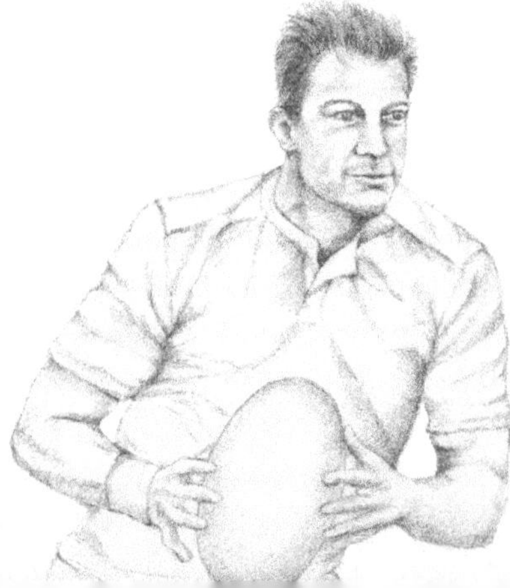

THREE HUNDRED AND TWENTY-ONE DAYS

They say that every cloud has a silver lining,
That just might be true for us, here, in the U.K.,
We've been a dark spot on the Covid map for months now,
Infection rates rampant, second only to the U.S.A.

We've been saturated by the virus and its variants,
We've had Alpha, we've had Delta, and the rest,
It's been lurking everywhere, unaware that it's not wanted,
Like an uninvited, annoying party guest.

The number of daily cases has kept on climbing,
But the upside is, our immunity levels are rising too,
The constant bombardment means we're becoming more resistant,
The vaccination booster programme helping us get through.

It's not over but Covid cases are declining,
We're nearing 'endemic equilibrium', scientists say,
That sounds impressive; I think it means we're stable,
I'll take it as a positive, anyway!

There is a serious problem in Europe,
As a fourth wave of the virus sweeps in from the East,
Unlike here, infection rates have been low since the summer,
They thought it was all over; they became complacent, to say the least.

They were too quick to scale back on Covid measures,
Track and trace was suspended, they thought the booster programme could wait,
People stopped presenting themselves for vaccination,
Governments realise their mistakes but is it too late?

Suddenly, there's a sense of urgency, even panic,
As Europe is labelled the 'epicentre' of infection once more,
Severe restrictions have been imposed, including Covid passes,
Compulsory vaccinations, evening curfews and lockdowns, like before.

But, this time, many people are not conforming,
It's a 'Coronavirus dictatorship', they say, and they're ready to protest,
The 'anti-vaxers' are out in force, and the human rights defenders,
As they invade the city streets, they're causing riots and unrest.

They are fighting for their dignity, I understand it,
Like me, they are furious and resentful, but they'll not win,
After twenty months, for them, it is no better,
But I think they should do what I've done, and just give in!

Now a new variant has emerged out in South Africa!
It's already strayed into Botswana, Belgium, Israel, and Hong Kong,
We thought Delta was bad enough, but Omicron is stronger,
They think it might be resistant to our defences; I hope they're
wrong.

So, the fight continues, and the scientists are counter-punching,
They'll just 'adapt the vaccine'! That's so impressive, I must say,
Covid is surging across Europe, but we're not complacent,
This new strain will arrive here soon, I'm sure; it's on its way!

THREE HUNDRED AND FORTY-TWO DAYS

There's a bit of turbulence in the Government's cockpit at the moment,
It's a bumpy ride for the Prime Minister and his crew,
Accusations are being hurled through the air towards them,
Denials of elitism are being made, but are they true?

Apparently, there was an issue near Christmas 2020,
They told us not to celebrate, 'you're in tier three, you must obey',
But it seems those Conservative politicians had a party,
They didn't let the Covid regulations stand in their way.

When challenged, they maintained it didn't happen,
But, 'If it did, no rules were broken', so that is fine,
'It was just cheese and wine, a business meeting', said an advisor,
But her disdain showed through, it was inevitable, she must resign.

Leaked video footage was the undoing of Allegra Stratton,
She joked about a cover-up to hide their 'crime',
She appeared arrogant and disrespectful, which is quite worrying,
As she was the Government's main spokesperson at the time.

She was very tearful as she apologised for her behaviour,
'I will regret those remarks', she said, 'for the rest of my days',
Once again, a parliamentary aide abusing privilege,
When will it be, that people in politics change their ways?

'Planet Boris is the strangest place in the world',
A cabinet minister said a few days ago,
'No rules apply there' and 'he's able to defy gravity',
A special talent, which stops him from sinking too low.

He's been stumbling along, surviving all the disasters,
He has tripped up a few times, and still he comes through,
But now, there are rumblings amongst ministers and party members,
As the mistakes mount up and start to implicate them too.

There was the lobbying scandal and attempt to change regulations,
To protect a Tory MP as he was then,
The obscene cover stories to hide illegal Christmas parties,
And the lavish renovation of the flat at Number Ten.

The moderates of the Party are grumpy about his foreign policy,
The Brexiteers are cross that he is not being strong enough,
The constituency MP's say he is, 'all mouth and no trousers',
And the right wing want the human rights law changed; they've had
enough.

The feeling of discontent and frustration is tangible,
Some are convinced the PM is 'running out of road',
Yet, as usual, he appears to be indestructible,
But what about his planet? It's shuddering and could easily
implode…

Omicron has arrived in style for Christmas,
It's joining Delta, which is still determined to hang about,
Professor Whitty says, we must 'deprioritise certain social contacts',
I think that means, don't enjoy yourselves and don't go out!

The Prime Minister is desperately trying to be positive,
The booster jab programme is having an impact, he would say,
The daily infection rates are at the highest ever, so I doubt it,
But surely, this persistent nightmare has to end one day…

... Let's hope it's soon!

Sue Dower

www.ingramcontent.com/pod-product-compliance
Lightning Source LLC
Chambersburg PA
CBHW080333030726
47593CB00010B/2988